VIRGIN

LIFE CAN BE
POSITIVELY DIFFERENT

My Three Golden Keys to
Feeling More Positive

Order this book online at www.trafford.com
or email orders@trafford.com

Most Trafford titles are also available at major online book retailers.

Printed in the United States of America.

ISBN: 978-1-4120-7677-7 (sc)
ISBN: 978-1-4122-4013-0 (ebook)
ISBN: 978-1-4669-1588-6 (audio)

Trafford rev. 4/27/2012

 www.trafford.com

North America & international
toll-free: 1 888 232 4444 (USA & Canada)
phone: 250 383 6864 ♦ fax: 812 355 4082

CONTENTS

◯ PART 1 ◯

FEELING POSITIVE WITHIN YOURSELF

CHAPTER 1 ACCEPTING YOURSELF

CHAPTER 2 APPRECIATING YOURSELF

CHAPTER 3 SUPPORTING YOURSELF

∾ PART II ∾

RELATING POSITIVELY TO OTHERS

CHAPTER 4 ACCEPTING OTHERS

CHAPTER 5 APPRECIATING OTHERS

CHAPTER 6 SUPPORTING OTHERS

⟶ PART III ⟵
FEELING POSITIVE ABOUT LIFE

CHAPTER 7 FLOWING WITH LIFE

PREFACE

When I read the original version of my book for the purpose of doing an audio version, I felt like I had written an instruction manual, full of tips on how to live more positively. When I wrote it ten years ago, I think that I was not quite ready to share the more private details of my story with my readers. Now, I have come to realize that it is other people's stories that readers enjoy and value the most as they can relate or react to them based on their own story. Today, I share with you my story and mainly how I managed to cope positively during the many challenges I faced in the last fifty years.

When I trained in the martial arts, we were taught a large number of self-defense techniques. We were told that they were just ideas, possibilities from which we could tap from. They were not written in stone. What I wrote here, are just that, my ideas and thoughts based on what I have learned from my studies, my clients, my friends and family and my life. As you read on, you may come to reflect on your own outlook and circumstances. You may find that some are similar to mine and some are radically different. No matter what, my book will give you a chance to consider your approach to life compared to mine. You may even find some of the ideas or keys I bring up useful to you. I sure hope so.

As my son said to me jokingly a few days ago: "Life Can Be Positively Different and so can this book". May my story be of value in helping you live yours.

INTRODUCTION

When I was living in England, one morning as I was rushing out the door, I bumped into my neighbor and we exchanged the usual greetings. Then he asked me a question, which puzzled me for a long time afterwards. He said, "Virginia, how do you do it?" Confused I responded "How do I do what?" "How do you keep so positive all of the time?" All I answered was "chocolate, chocolate keeps me going". I had never really thought about what kept me so cheerful all the time. One thing I knew, I enjoyed chocolate and it was supposed to help you feel upbeat. His question remained with me for a while. I was baffled to find a deeper answer than the one I had come up with. Yes, chocolate had been a great mood lifter for me over the years but there had to be more than that. What was it?

I thought about the fact that when different people witness the same situation; they all give a different account of it. They all perceive life in their own unique way. Maybe the way I perceived my life and my circumstances helped me keep a positive approach. I definitely did not have a perfect life. At the time, I had recently divorced and was a single, working mother with two young children living in a country where I knew nobody. My mother had also been recently diagnosed with bone cancer. Life was far from easy and stress free for me back then.

So what kept me smiling through the hard times of my life? One day it just came to me, I held on to a positive and optimistic attitude and that kept me going. Digging even deeper, I found that my core beliefs greatly helped me in this approach. I had learned to accept that life is challenging and that the best I can do in difficult situations is to be resourceful and ride the wave. Not to say I did not feel like I was drowning many times along the way. I had also learned to be grateful for my blessings. I had made sure to keep focusing on the positives in my life and find solace in the fact that there were some. Finally, I had come to realize the importance of support especially from having experienced a lack of it. Supporting myself-being my best friend and life coach helped me cope.

In the end, these seemed to be the three golden keys for me-acceptance, appreciation and support. I realized as well that by offering those to others, you could have a beneficial impact on their lives. As a result of a benign conversation on a cold and wet doorstep one morning, I came to write this book to share my "golden keys"-the ones that allowed me to discover my own "wisdom treasure chest". This I where I go when I feel down, overwhelmed or discouraged.

If I bumped into my old neighbor today, this is what I would tell him: "to cope with all the upheavals in my life, my tumultuous childhood, my mentally unstable and emotionally unavailable mother, being raised by numerous caregivers, my moves across three continents, the loss of my two closest and dearest friends one to suicide at 31 and the other one after her long and horrendous battle against cancer at 37, my divorce and being a single working mother in yet another foreign country-I just had to keep hanging on for dear life to my "golden keys" and just hope that they would pull me through. I needed to "accept" that all the traumatic events in my life were part of the many lessons I needed to learn and that they helped me become a wiser and more compassionate person. I needed to "appreciate" the gifts in my life-the people I loved and who loved me, my wonderful children and my good health. I needed to keep "supporting" myself for I could only rely on myself overall to pull through all the difficult times in my life.

Therefore, I have used my keys numerous times over the years and today; I want to share them with you. Maybe you have found your own keys and they work for you. Maybe you are searching for some or need different ones now. No matter where you are in your journey, I hope that you may find some resources here that you can use to make your life positively different.

❧ PART 1 ❧

FEELING POSITIVE WITHIN YOURSELF

CHAPTER 1

ACCEPTING YOURSELF

BEING AWARE OF YOUR "CORE BELIEFS"

In my work as a therapist, I have heard many stories over the years. Every one of them was unique. What truly fascinated me about those stories was how the individuals in them perceived the challenges they faced and how they came to make sense of them in order to deal them.

What I realized over time was that their core beliefs about themselves and about their lives played a great role in how they came to interpret events. While I was living in New Zealand, I took a course in Neuro-Linguistic Programming. During the training, we learned specific techniques to change a person's beliefs. These were aimed at helping people let go of old limiting beliefs and replace them with new more beneficial ones.

Although when I took the course I had already finished my counseling studies and done much self-reflection as part of that training, I was stunned to discover how many negative beliefs I held about myself. I was also shocked to realize how much of an impact they had on how I viewed myself as a person. I was far from accepting myself back then and in dire need of more than a few belief changes.

Learning those useful techniques meant opening the door to another universe. I was completely unaware of how differently I could think and feel once I modified how I perceived myself. Needless to say, I was thrilled by the changes I underwent. I was more than eager to share my new discovery with anyone willing to listen and give it a try. Some of my clients experienced deep changes as result of letting go of their old beliefs and embracing new ones.

One of my clients, who had worked on changing some of his beliefs, gave me some feedback on how it had improved his life when I saw him a year after he stopped coming to me. He updated me on his life and was extremely grateful for the work he had done on himself. He actually looked and acted very differently. He seemed to have blossomed as a result. I was thrilled. He told me that he had turned his life around. He was planning on leaving his unhappy marriage and pursue the career he had always wanted. He was also taking better care of himself and enjoying life more.

To transform our lives for the better, we need to be ready to change. It takes work and also has many repercussions in all areas of our existence. The people around us may be taken back by the changes in us and some may not welcome them wholeheartedly. When I altered my belief about being "loveable", I no longer agreed with my mother's view of me and that caused much friction between us. She was not ready for me to be my own person. For me on the other hand, the change was long overdue.

Are you prepared to make big changes or are you looking at small alterations? Once you switch your perspective, many unforeseen things can happen.

Some of my clients, to whom I suggested looking into how their belief system may be hampering their attempts to live the life they were seeking, were skeptical or concerned about altering how their minds worked for them. Some were scared of making changes in their lives or did not feel ready to do so. I always respected the fact that the choice was theirs to make.

YOUR BELIEF SYSTEM

Many of our beliefs are developed during childhood while we learn about the world around us. Our parents have their own belief systems and we tend to absorb many of their values as we live in their world. It is worth taking a few minutes to reflect on what beliefs you developed over the years and how they affected how you perceive yourself and your life. The many interactions you have had with people over time have shaped how you view yourself today. Judgments or comments made by our parents or our schoolteachers can become very strong labels for us and have an impact on us throughout our lives.

My mother disliked the fact that I was a tomboy as a child and used to call me a "brute". Thinking back, her derogatory comments affected my perception of my femininity adversely later on. We tend to internalize how others perceive us especially when we are young and highly receptive to our family input.

Negative descriptions of ourselves can wound our self-image and lead us to feel a lesser person for it.

Becoming aware of all the labels that have been attached to you throughout your life by your parents, your teachers or your lovers, is the first step to changing how you view yourself. It enables you to disconnect from how others see you and take an honest look at how much of how you perceive yourself comes from them, not you. You may want to take a moment to think about the kind of attributes you would use to describe yourself and where they come from. Can you trace them back to an event or a comment? Are those attributes truly descriptive of you or just someone else's interpretation or criticism that you have internalized?

LOOKING BACK

Some images and words from our past stick in our minds so clearly. It is like they still live inside of us as powerfully as when they actually happened. Those vivid recollections usually have quite an emotional charge to them. The intense feelings attached to those memories keep them real in our minds.

Remembering your first memory as a child can be quite enlightening. My first one was of being in an elevator surrounded by doctors who were taking me to the operating room to have my tonsils removed. I was about 2 or 3 years old and had no idea what was happening to me. The picture is as clear in my mind now as if it were today. The feeling I had is still strong-I was going to die. This first recollection has affected greatly my attitude towards my health and how I manage it.

What about you? What are some of your most powerful childhood and adulthood memories? How have they shaped you? Do you still hear your mother's or father's words telling you that you are a certain way or that your life is meant to be a certain way? Have these comments been helpful to you or have they caused you not to live the life you wanted to have or be the person you wanted to be? Take some time to remember and notice and how you have taken them on board.

LETTING GO OF OLD BELIEFS

It always amazes me how much easier it has been for me to hold on to old negative beliefs than to embrace new positive ones. When your self-image has been molded by a very strict and judgmental upbringing, the years of absorbing negative comments do not just fade easily or quickly. It has taken me years to come to terms and release most of my negative beliefs.

There is a wonderful saying by Jonas Salk that goes like this: "Good parents give their children roots and wings. Roots to know where home is, wings to fly away and exercise what's been taught to them". To feel like you have strong and deep roots, you need to have been nurtured as a child. To grow those roots that will sustain you through life, you need to have been loved and encouraged. Then, you can truly stand on your own two feet and feel that you matter as an individual. Then once you do get your wings, you will be confident and self-assured enough to believe that you can fly.

My roots were very thin when I flew away before finishing high school. It made my flight much more precarious and challenging. How are your roots? Are they healthy and deeply planted or tangled and exposed? It may be impossible to go back and change how your roots were originally taken care of. Yet, you can strengthen the ones you have now. You can build up your self-image by creating new "positive beliefs" that will make you feel stronger.

What are some new beliefs you would like to adopt? Have you identified the ones that are holding you back or making you feel insecure? They are the ones that you wish you could let go of in order to feel good about yourself and feel confident about following your dreams. Those limiting ideas we hang on to are usually associated with fear-fear of not being good enough, fear of failure, fear of embarrassment and fear of being judged. What are your fears? What are the thoughts associated with them?

To let go of those negative thoughts and emotions that are hindering your life, you need to become aware of them-expose them once and for all. It took me a very long time to finally admit my fear of rejection and of being alone. My fears were based on my experiences with my mother and led me to believe that I was neither loveable nor deserving to be cared for. Those beliefs were so engrained in me that they motivated me to make decisions in my life that harmed me. Those decisions were based on these deep-seated beliefs and the fear they created. They had nothing to do with who I truly was as a person yet I could not realize that.

Letting go of negative thoughts and deep fears can be a difficult and lengthy process. Yet, letting go of them will set you free-free to be content with who you are and have a more fulfilling life.

EMBRACING NEW POSITIVE BELIEFS

Although switching your mindset does not happen overnight, it is possible. Our minds have amazing ways of learning new things and maturing with time. As our experience of life changes, we grow wiser. As I mentioned earlier, there are specific techniques that I learned during my NLP training which can help you change your beliefs. On your own, using visualizations and positive affirmations can be beneficial to help you adopt new ways of perceiving yourself and your life. Many books have been written on those topics.

Another technique I have found very useful in the past is to reframe the way you approach yourself or situations in your life. I have caught myself many times criticizing myself harshly or going down "pity lane". It has taken great effort on my part to catch myself and reframe my negative internal comments or my perspective on my circumstances. Over and over again, I had to make a point of switching my thinking from negative to positive.

At first, constantly reframing everything can seem overwhelming and the benefits of it unrealistic. Yet with time, it does become easier and you find out of the blue that your outlook has shifted. The more you reframe, the more you recondition yourself to think differently. You create new grooves in your brain and bypass the "old negative ones". Ultimately, the goal is to rewire yourself in order to create a whole new set of "positive beliefs" that supersedes the old one.

When I finally felt confident in my new belief of being loveable in spite of my mother's treatment and comments, I expressed my new outlook to her. I was finally able to communicate my unwillingness to be someone I was not or become someone I never wanted to be just to be loved by the one person who was meant to love me regardless. I no longer needed her love nor her approval to feel worthy and I felt incredibly relieved. I was free at last to be "me" not the ideal picture of me someone else had created to fulfill their own lives.

I was left to confront my guilt for letting her down but I soon realize that my guilt was unwarranted. I was now faced with making my own choices regardless of what others thought. I was going to rely on my own wisdom. I came to the conclusion that only you can live in your skin and fulfill your destiny. Letting others dictate those for you will only lead to resentment and much inner turmoil.

DROPPING SELF-IMPOSED PRESSURES

I grew up in a world built on strict rules and behavioral guidelines. There were rules for everything-how to look, dress, act, speak, conduct yourself in private and in public. These endless rules were the pillars of my upbringing. The ones that seem most difficult to bear were the unspoken ones. Those haunted me as a child. They came from the expectations my family had of me. The pressure always lived inside of me causing me much stress and anxiety. I felt like if I did not live up to these crucial expectations, I was committing a major crime-disappointing my family. It meant being perfect all of the time-always saying the right thing or not saying the wrong thing, behaving flawlessly. It also meant living with the constant fear of letting my parents down.

Pressuring ourselves to be someone we are not or act in a way that is not natural to us can cause us a great deal of unnecessary stress. By dropping those pressures and embracing ourselves for who we are, we allow ourselves to be authentic and fulfill our potential. It opens a whole world of possibilities free of constraints and restrictions. We can now drop the "shoulds", "ought tos", "need tos", "have tos" and switch to the "want tos" and "seek tos". We are no longer burdened by having to live up to expectations that can lead to undue frustrations and disappointments.

Forcing ourselves to change can also really dampen our spirit. Often in relationships, one or both partners live in the hope that the other one will change. They may think that if he or she loves them, they will change for them. I have learned that people will not change unless they truly want to and it can cause a great deal of friction to expect someone else to do so for us. Trying to be different from who we are can be extremely taxing and reduce our ability to enjoy life. In the end, it is acceptance that opens us up to new horizons, to a new "freedom from" pressures; and to a new "freedom to" enjoy a more flowing and positive life.

ACCEPTANCE-THE PATH TO INNER PEACE & CONTENTMENT

I used to think that accepting myself meant resigning myself to the fact that I could not change who I was and what happened in my life. I was wrong and right at the same time. I have changed a great deal over the years-mostly working on my beliefs, my fears and how I deal with my circumstances. In that respect, I was mistaken. However, I was right in the sense that there are fundamental physical attributes we cannot change such as our height or the color of our eyes or certain circumstances such as when we were born and the family we were born into. Some things we do inherit and we do have to accept to live with them.

To find inner-peace, we need to be able to live with who we are everyday of our lives. Comparing ourselves to others or to who we "could" have been will cause us much strife in the end. There are many things about myself I wish were different. Playing the movie of my life back, I often imagine other scenarios. I could have been a very different person and chosen different paths. There were many crossroads in my life, sometimes I feel like I took the wrong path-the harder and more obscure one. In order to accept myself, I had to come to terms with all the decisions I made over the years and put them in perspective.

Who I am today would do things differently. But it is thanks to all those learning experiences that I am this person I have become. I cannot rewrite my past; only accept it for all the lessons it offered and for how it helped me grow. By dropping any judgments, regrets and remorse I have been able to free myself and make peace with myself. By accepting who I used to be and who I am now, I have become more tolerant of others as well and of their unfolding development.

CHAPTER 2

APPRECIATING YOURSELF

APPRECATIATING ALL THAT YOU ARE

At birth, we come into the world with a body, a mind, a heart and a spirit. For the rest of our days, we live with them all of the time. As the years go by, we become accustomed to how they function and how they keep changing. Our bodies keep maturing and transforming, our minds get filled with thoughts, ideas and memories, knowledge and wisdom, our hearts experience love, joy, sadness and loss and our spirit guides us throughout. During all that time, we rarely stop and think about how they serve us until they cause us some pain.

When I took a class in physiology, I was amazed to discover how complex the functioning of our body is. So many systems are at work. We are like an intricate and efficient machine operating every day and night without even realizing it. Becoming aware of this thrilled me, as I came to appreciate how wondrous human beings truly are. It is miraculous how all our organs go about fulfilling their comprehensive tasks for us on a daily basis. That alone is something to be grateful for.

When I gave birth to my children, I could not believe that my body was able to produce a replica of me. Inside of me lived a factory that could create life. That was mesmerizing to me. I remember reading many books on pregnancy while I was expecting and feeling a sense of amazement at how perfectly everything unfolded to create a new life. Often times, I look at my children today baffled by the fact that I carried them around for those nine months while they were getting ready to come into the world. I am truly grateful for the lives that were created inside of me and to my body for bringing two wonderful human beings into my life.

I am thankful for my health everyday and although my mind and my heart have gone through much pain in the past, I am still grateful that they have been part of my learning experience on this earth. Both my mind and my heart have matured and grown gentler and wiser with the passing years.

MAKING PEACE WITH YOUR MIND

My mind has often been my worse enemy. Making friend with it has been a life long process. Filled with negative thoughts from my past, I often struggled with feeling positive about myself. Negative self-talk can really take its toll on you as you live in your head every single day. It can lead to severe depression, low self-image and a long list of life-debilitating states of mind. It has taken me a long time to realize that I was in charge of my thoughts and that I could therefore choose to think differently.

When I decided to make peace with my mind, I made sure to become mindful of all of my ideas and how they affected me. I took notice of them. I decided to switch my self-talk. It took me a while to believe that I could have mostly positive thoughts and that they could match my reality. I began to polish my mind into a clear prism so that it could create rainbows instead of thunderstorms.

Once, when I was visiting a friend at the end of her life, she looked at me caringly and said, as she reached over for what seemed to be a plain rock: "this is how you see yourself". Then she turned the rock over to reveal a beautiful amethyst and added: "this is who you truly are". I believe that inside all of us lives an amethyst that we may or may not have yet acknowledged. We all have the ability to uncover it and keep shining it.

There is so much undiscovered beauty lying beneath the surface. Once you recognize it, your whole way of looking at yourself will shift. You will become grateful for being unique and beautiful.

SURROUND YOURSELF WITH PEOPLE WHO APPRECIATE YOU

Who we are friends with not only says a great deal about us, it also affects us in many ways. Have you ever noticed how some people make you feel really good about yourself? These people tend to have a positive and appreciative approach to life and it rubs off on you. When we are in a group, our brains actually connect with each other and influence one another. The limbic part of our brain, which regulates emotions, communicates with others around to match the mood of whatever situation you are in. That is why, when you walk into a lively party, you feel uplifted. Meanwhile, during a funeral, you will feel sad even if you did not know the person who passed. Moods are literally contagious.

Because of how affected we are by people when we are in direct contact with them, who we surround ourselves with becomes crucial to how we feel. Once we have become more positive in our own outlook, individuals with negative mindsets can become difficult to be around. We may no longer feel comfortable around them and be pulled towards people who match our new state more. The good news is that people who appreciate you and your new perception, will reinforce it. Others may not be as open to it or even resent the fact that you have found a way to enjoy life more while they are stuck in old ineffective patterns.

You now have a choice to make. You can hang on to some relationships that pull you down or decide to surround yourself strictly with friends who make you feel positive. Some of my friendships have faded over the years mostly because we found no longer had anything in common or we were no longer on the same wavelength. Although it was often sad to realize, I came to terms with the fact that different individuals grow and change at varying pace and in sometimes-divergent directions over the years. It just is the way it is.

Hanging on to things or people just because of our fear of letting go can become counter-productive and keep us from growing. Take a moment to think about the people who surround you.

How do they make you feel? Do you feel positive and energized around them or negative and drained? It is worth noticing for you have a choice with whom you associate.

A STATE OF GRATITUDE

When attending a seminar on the treatment of traumas this week, I was reminded by one of the presenters how beneficial gratitude can be for individuals who suffer from depression. Research has shown how counting your blessings everyday can greatly lift your spirits. After only one month of being grateful every night for as little as five things in their lives, depressed people had greatly improved. As one of my professors said repeatedly to us in graduate school "you can't feel good and bad at the same time".

Twenty years ago, I was very comforted by how much feeling grateful could improve how I felt. I had just read the book Louise Hay had edited called "Gratitude-A Way of Life". Many different writers had shared what gratitude meant to them and how being grateful had benefitted their lives. I found the observations of metaphysical teacher Daniel Peralta's particularly helpful; he wrote, "Gratitude focuses our attention on the good things in life. It takes our blessings and multiplies them. When we joyfully express appreciation, it opens our hearts and allows us to experience more love."

For me, gratitude means a positive reverence for everything. When my world seemed to be crashing down, that was the thread that I held onto. I would look at the beauty of the trees and the flowers in my garden, at my loving dog lying at my feet, at the angelic faces of my children while they were sleeping and I would feel this deep feeling of appreciation. Reminding myself of the things and people I loved brought me back to a place where I felt true gratitude.

Even at times when our circumstances and the people around us may not seem to warrant much gratitude, I have found that looking for the silver lining can be helpful. Finding something positive in a difficult situation can make it more bearable. I do not mean that you should remain in bad situations and just put up with them. At times though, challenges cannot be avoided and how we ride the wave does make a difference for us.

In certain cases in my life, it has been most difficult for me to find the silver lining in what happened. The passing of my two best friends left such a void in my existence that I could not come up with anything positive at first to make sense of the loss or cope with it. In the end, I came back to my other key-acceptance. I just had to accept that they were gone and I had to keep living with out them. Then, I became conscious of the fact that them going meant that they would no longer be suffering and for that I was truly grateful. It is heartbreaking to watch people you love in pain whether it is physical, mental or emotional. Although I still miss them everyday, I am glad that they are free of pain and that is the silver lining.

BEAUTY IS IN THE EYE OF THE BEHOLDER

I have always enjoyed photography. Taking photos meant immortalizing the beauty around me. I could hold onto a space or time that had great value to me. I could have the happy pieces of my life forever on a sheet of photo paper. I took endless photos as a teenager and in my youth. Behind my camera lens, I knew I could find beauty in the most unexpected places-in a building reflected in a puddle or in the smile of a playing child. By appreciating all of the beauty that surrounded me, I felt more alive, more a part of something bigger and wondrous. Life just seemed magnificent.

When you have experienced a great amount of negativity in your life such as criticisms and judgments from others, it can be difficult to recognize your inner beauty. Our self-talk is filled with negative thoughts about ourselves. We still hear harsh comments in our heads, which make us feel less than wonderful. We have internalized those putdowns and they have shaped our self-image. In order to feel more positive about ourselves then, we have to counterbalance them. We need to polish that gem inside of us.

In order to do so, we need to look below the surface and start digging into who we are. If you were asked to come up with some of your most positive attributes, what would they be? Write them all down. Were you aware of them? Did you give them credit? This list can be a valuable reminder in the future when you are feeling low or doubting yourself of how valuable you truly are.

NO MORE COMPARING-YOU ARE UNIQUE

When we are not feeling good or things are not going well in our lives, we may look around us and feel like others have more to offer than us or have better lives. We may think, if only I could be more like them or have what they have, then, my life would be so much better. I have gone through this tempting logic a few times. I was actually surprised and somewhat comforted to find out that other people's personalities and circumstances were just as challenging if not more than mine. Wondering if I would trade my life with any of them, I came to the conclusion that I would not. This effort to find a better life besides mine led me to some valuable insights.

It occurred to me that we all have strengths and weaknesses. We all live through difficult times. We all have trouble coping at some point in our lives. We all try to find the best way we know to deal with our challenges and we all learn and grow from those experiences. In the end, I recognized that except for the purpose of this realization, comparing ourselves to others was ludicrous. We are all completely different and unique and so are our circumstances.

Because we cannot switch life with anyone else, enjoying ours becomes crucial. As Bob Marley sang: "You can't run away from yourself."

Once we acknowledge and accept the fact that we have our own set of characteristics and our own situations to live with, we can focus on improving both who we are as a person and the conditions we are currently experiencing. Also, by making sure that you appreciate yourself for who you are, you can find the joy and peace in being you.

YOUR LIFE STARTS NOW

There are many beginnings in life. They are markers in our lives, which symbolize the end of a phase and the start of a new one. Beginnings bring with them wonderful opportunities to reach for new goals and embrace new ways of doing things. They can be full of hopes and dreams. They can make us feel alive. I have had many of those-new lives beginning in different places with different people. Every time, I felt a little apprehensive about how things would turn out, how I would cope. Ultimately, I would tell myself that a new beginning was a chance to create a new and better life for myself, to reach for those stars I always gazed at from afar. I was just launching out on a new adventure and I was the hero in my story. Everything was possible.

As Goethe wrote over two hundred years ago: "Whatever you can do or dream you can, begin it. Boldness has genius, power and magic in it". Now is the time for you to begin whatever you have been dreaming of. As they say "the present" is a gift." It is a gift you give to yourself as only you can live your life right now wherever you are. Now is an important moment as it sets the mood for the rest of your life. Now is your chance. Of course, there will be other "nows", actually many others. The opportunity to create a life of joy and appreciation will present itself to you over and over again but why not start now? It is never too late but it's never too early either-the choice is yours.

There may be many reasons why your life seems hard to enjoy right now. You may be faced with serious challenges that make it difficult for you to appreciate all life has to offer. You may not feel up to anything bold or different. Appreciating anything may seem farfetched yet remember to honor your feelings and appreciate yourself for in the face of adversity, you are hanging on. You are riding the wave the best you can even if your best does not feel that great right now. Have compassion for yourself and remember that as Annie said in the musical that bears her name "the sun will come out tomorrow". If now seems hard, don't give up on yourself for there will be better days.

You will find eventually that once you have developed a sense of appreciation for yourself and treated yourself with compassion, you will also be able to do the same for others. You will come to realize that others struggle with challenges just like you do and that they deserve the same kind of treatment: understanding and appreciation; for being human means facing numerous trials and tribulations. We are all in the same boat.

CHAPTER 3

SUPPORTING YOURSELF

HOW DO WE SUPPORT OURSELVES?

Our skeleton has this amazing ability to hold our body erect and protect all of our organs. Our body has its own support system and every part of it supports one another. What about our minds and our hearts, what are the innate supports that we possess to keep them functioning at their highest potential and serving us the best they can? When we are born, our brain, unlike other organs is not fully formed. The parts of our brain that regulate our thoughts and emotions have not developed to their mature state. This means that they are vulnerable and malleable. The way our minds and hearts are nurtured during the many experiences we have in our lives will determine how well they function.

How have you learned to use your mind and your heart-to help you or to hurt you? Are your thoughts supporting you or working against you? Is your heart filled with hope and love or sorrow and resentment? What do you do to support yourself? What do you do when you are hurting? Do you put yourself down or do you act like a caring friend? Very few of us learn how to deal with hard times constructively and effectively from a young age. We tend to reproduce our parents' coping mechanisms. Some of us may take out our distress on others like we watched our parents do. Others may hide in their shell as they learned from a parent. Some may try self-medicating by reaching for an alcoholic drink, a mind-altering substance or comfort foods to alleviate the pain. Destructive behaviors are common ways of dealing with one's pain yet make our troubles even worse.

Now, imagine that you had the mental and emotional skills to support a friend in need-you would reach out and offer a helping hand. You would be there for them, encouraging them with positive and constructive words. You would remain calm and comforting, reminding them that they were going through a difficult time and that they could count on you to be there for them. This is the friend you need inside yourself to help you weather the challenges in your life.

We all face trials at some point and we need to develop positive strategies to deal with them. Rallying our minds and emotions to help us through will make coping that much easier. Many therapies offer helpful techniques to develop positive mental and emotional skills. I was fortunate enough to be exposed to Life Skills classes, which were developed as part of Marsha Linehan's Dialectical Behavioral Therapy. I found the skills she taught extremely helpful to identify and manage our mental and emotional responses. As I was learning these skills, I remember thinking "if only everyone was taught how to do this from a young age, we would be so much better equipped to deal with life and all its tribulations".

Knowing how to support ourselves, requires some skill and much compassion. Developing those can help us become more resourceful in the way we tackle situations and live a more peaceful and joyful life.

SOME DAYS LIFE SEEMS TO RESIST

We have all had the kinds of days where we just feel like staying in bed and letting the world go by. Days, where we do not have it in us to face whatever is going on in our lives. In my teen years, I experienced that feeling a great deal and wondered often how things could get better. Life just seemed to resist me with overpowering force. I felt like the fight would require more strength than I had at the time-mentally and emotionally. I then came to realize that if anyone were going to pull myself out of that dark hole I felt buried in, it would have to be me. I would have to find the inner resources I did not know I had to climb out and embrace life again.

So how do we cope when life seems to resist? We all have different ways. Some are more constructive than others though. Distracting ourselves from our state can be helpful especially if it is through positive activities such as sports, movies or reading. Eventually, we will need to become engaged again and deal with whatever is going on. We can choose to be on our side and support ourselves as well as ask for outside help. In the end though, we need to do the work to pull ourselves out. Only we can turn our lives around. Only we can live in our mind and in our heart.

For me, it meant getting out of a bad situation and starting a new life far away. I gave myself another chance in life by taking risks, getting out of my comfort zone and believing that I could have a better life. It took all I had left to launch yet staying would have caused my demise. Sometimes, you need to make radical changes and hang onto the sliver of hope that still lives inside of you that things can get better.

In the overall scheme of things, we also have to accept that life takes us through all seasons and weathers and at times all we can do is ride the wave. As Jung wrote: "Even a happy life cannot be without a measure of darkness, and the word "happiness" would lose its meaning if it were not balanced by sadness". How we treat ourselves through the moments of sadness is what can make the difference between misery and sadness. If we take it out on ourselves or on others, we make things worse. When we are gentle and supportive of ourselves during the tough times, we develop compassion and caring for ourselves. We choose to use our mind and our heart positively.

Ultimately, you cannot always change the circumstances in your life but you always have a choice on how you deal with them. You can feel victimized and drown partly in your own sorrows or you can attempt to ride the surf.

GO WITH THE FLOW

One of my favorite stories as a child was about a reed and the old oak. When a storm hit, the reed bent in the wind and just "went with the flow". It remained flexible. As a result, it survived the storm. Meanwhile, the strong, old tree stood up to the wind and fought it with all its might. As a result of its rigidity, it broke. That story stayed with me through life especially when I resisted with all my might and realized I was hurting myself by doing so. I believed that strength would pull me through; I was like that old oak. Life has taught me over and over again to be flexible. Becoming a reed took a long time but fortunately I have grown wiser with the passing years.

When I read what Joseph Chilton Pearce wrote about going with the flow, it hit home:

> *To enter an unpredictable situation and accept it openly is*
> *to flow with its energy, be augmented in your own energy*
> *and relax its stresses and tensions accordingly.*

I have learned that the more I tend to resist a situation, the more it resists as well. A great deal of energy is wasted in the process. It would appear that rigidity tends to lead to more rigidity while flexibility allows for more possibilities to appear. In the end, a flexible mind and open heart will take you a long way, as you remain light and pliable through life. Have you ever noticed how when you force things to happen, they just don't turn out for the best? So be aware of how your life is flowing and just let it be. You will find the challenges will become easier and less dramatic.

How many times have I gotten stressed out in my car because I was stuck in a traffic jam or behind a slow car when I was in a rush? I had the choice to honk my horn, scream at the driver in front of me, tailgate him or her-all pretty ineffective and energy-consuming options or I could listen to some good music, take a few deep breaths, look around at the trees or the street and just make the best of a stressful situation. Now, if I had picked the first option, I would be feeling even more tense, the driver in front of me would be annoyed and angry with me and I may have even get into an accident. If I go for choice number two-I learn to manage my nervous tension, diffuse any potential mishaps involving other drivers and arrive at my destination no faster yet more calm and peaceful.

Remaining flexible and composed at all times is not always easy. I will admit I have lost my cool in more than one occasion. When my children were little and they were fighting, when it got the better of me, I used to go into the bathroom and tell myself to take three long deep breaths. It would calm me down and I would be able to deal with the situation much more effectively. Now that they are older, they remind to breathe when I get tense, they both say jokingly "mom, breathe". It makes me laugh and I realize that I am getting too worked up over something. I am glad that they remember my "diffusion technique" and have learned a positive way to calm down. Funnily enough, they now use it on me.

Over the years, I have found that when you keep an open and serene mind, events tend to flow more easily and in a better direction. When we put up a fight and resist, we attract more resistance. The path of least resistance definitely seems to bring us the most serenity and contentment. By sticking to set expectations and beliefs about how things should be or should turn out, we tend to limit our options and our adaptability to various situations.

ZOOM OUT

As a photographer, I used to love using the zoom on my camera. It allowed me to get really close to my subject or to have some distance from it without moving at all. From the same spot, I could get different views. As much as I liked switching on the macro option and being able to see all the details of a flower or of an insect, by doing so I had no perspective on it. It took up the whole frame. I could not put it into context anymore. What I had magnified by zooming in was all that there was. I have discovered that in our lives the same thing tends to apply, when we are standing too close to someone or to a situation, we have difficulty putting things into context. They take the whole space in our minds.

It is often hard to be objective when caught up in a muddled situation.

When challenges crop up in our lives, by zooming out and reframing our circumstances to look at the larger context and from a different angle, we can achieve a wider and alternative perspective on things. A similar technique I have found useful is to imagine that you are an outsider looking at your situation from afar. What does it look like to them? Emotionally detaching from our circumstances can help us de-dramatize our outlook and stay more composed. Try to picture how you would think about your current situation in a few months or years once its emotional impact has lessened. As we gain perspective and understanding, the emotional charge of events seem to fade and it makes them easier to cope with.

Time helps us get a better view on things and we often laugh later about events that seemed so dramatic at the time. Looking for the humor in a situation or for the silver lining can also alleviate some of our mental and emotional struggles. As a parent, I have found myself in plenty of tricky situations and my sense of humor has been a great tool in many of those. When my son was little and he would innocently asked embarrassing questions at the top of his voice in the middle of the supermarket or when my daughter poured out a whole bottle of bubble bath in the hot tub and turned on the jets when she was six, I just had to remind myself to look on the funny side and deal with those situations with good humor and calm. Parenthood is just full of trying times and keeping it light or "not sweating the small stuff" can save a great deal of our sanity.

I realize that at times, trying to find the funny side to our circumstances is not appropriate or possible. However, if it is suitable and you can find a comic angle, it may help you lighten up to some degree. Once you do, you often find also that others will react more positively as well.

YOU CAN'T TAKE IT WITH YOU

We come into the world with nothing and leave the same way. All of our material possessions mean nothing when we go. There is an old Frank Capra movie I really like called "You Can't Take It With You". I think that it really puts our tendency to get attached to things into perspective. Whether it is physical attributes or material possessions, it is a fact that when it is our time to leave this life, we can't take them with us. Although maintaining good health or being able to sustain ourselves financially are important factors in feeling well and secure, being too attached to them can lead to frustrations and discontentment.

As Capra showed, finding joy in the simple things in life and making the most of everyday is the recipe for living happily and fully. Appreciating the beauty around us, in the people we love, in art and music or in the natural world can bring us endless satisfaction.

When people look back at their lives towards the end of it, they rarely wish they had spent more time at the office or watching television. When Jack Canfield and Mark Victor Hansen interviewed elderly and terminally ill individuals for their book *Chicken Soup For The Soul*, the interviewees reported not so much having regrets for the things they had done but rather for the things they had not done.

An eighty five year old woman made the following comments: "If I had to do it again, I would travel lighter next time. If I had my life to live over, I would start barefoot earlier in the spring and stay that way later in the fall. I would go to more dances. I would ride more merry-go-rounds. I would pick more daisies." What do you think you will say when reflecting on your life at that age? Will you wish you had had more fun and appreciation for your life and the people in it? As I get older and I realize my time on this earth is shrinking, I make a point of enjoying each moment. When the time for me to go comes, I want to look back thinking: I loved as much as I could love and I found joy wherever I could. I truly gave life my all. Then, I think I will be happy to let it all go.

When I have had conversations with people at the end of their lives, many seemed to have become softer, more in tune with what their life could have been if they had listened more to their heart and less to their minds. Which one are you listening to?

INCREASE THE POSITIVES IN YOUR LIFE

When I look at my life now and make a list of the positives versus the negatives, I come up with a longer list of positives. It did not use to look like this for many reasons, some internal and others external. Part of why I was feeling negative was due to my challenging circumstances; another part was how I handled the difficult situations and people in my life. Some of the challenges I faced I had no control over. Some, however, I did and if I were to tackle them again, I would do it differently. In both cases, the one thing I did have control over was my attitude towards them. The negatives that I could have improved on were the ones that lived inside of me. I could have most definitely increased the positives by dealing with those. The fears, guilt and sadness that we carry around can create many negatives in our lives. They can be a starting point to help you feel more positive in general.

Letting go of negative emotions or situations can improve our quality of life immensely. On the other hand, increasing the things we enjoy in life can also improve it drastically. Those vary between people. Walking in nature, playing the saxophone, spending time with my children and friends, listening to music, taking photos or discovering new places are uplifting to me. Now, what do you enjoy? What lifts your spirits? I should mention here that overindulging or engaging recklessly in activities that make us feel good could be counter-productive and bring long-term negatives to very short-term positives.

Moderation is, as always, the key. Anything can be overdone or pushed to extremes. By learning our limits and being able to recognize what can be destructive for us, we can enjoy the benefits of what brings us joy without incurring any detrimental consequences. In one of my social psychology classes in college, I was fascinated to learn about the "satiation principle". It just made so much sense to me. It demonstrated that the more you indulge in something, the less pleasurable it becomes. For example, the first bite of a chocolate cake is the most enjoyable one. As you eat more and more, each bite becomes less pleasant until you reach the point where you are satiated and can no longer take anymore. Past this point, eating more will make you feel sick and turn into an unpleasant experience.

Now, when you think about the amount of pleasant and enjoyable activities there are in your life right now, do they outweigh the more unpleasant ones? Could you somehow increase the more pleasurable ones? It might mean doing some reorganizing. It is amazing though how even a half hour per day of an enjoyable activity can improve our quality of life. I have personally found that a short walk in nature gives me the space to put my life in perspective and recharge my batteries. What is the one thing you could add to your day to improve it?

Children's ability to live in the moment and find even the simplest things fun has always amazed me. It is so refreshing. They have an innate knowing of how to enjoy themselves. Somehow, a lot of us have lost that ability as part of "growing up" and "maturing". Being childlike, innocent and enthusiastic can do wonders for our spirits. Jumping in puddles, singing to the top of our lungs, playing with colored crayons or just having a pillow fight can be plain rejuvenating and exhilarating fun. Borrow a child's eyes to rediscover the amazement of participating in all the wonders of our lives and our environment.

GO FOR YOUR DREAMS

When I was asked to come up with a quote to put under my senior photo for the high school yearbook, I picked the title of one of Aerosmith's song I particularly liked called "Dream On". The chorus goes "Dream until your dreams come true". I had a dream of being a foreign correspondent and telling the stories of the world. To achieve my dream, I went to college and studied politics thinking that I needed to know first what was going on in the world. My dream of being a writer did come true yet not quite as I imagined. I discovered along the way other interests and passions. I became a writer in the health field instead and found out that it suited me better. My aspiration to help others was more fulfilled in that field. It also led me to pursue degrees in counseling and now my Ph.D in Psychology.

No matter where your dreams take you. You have to start somewhere.

One of my Neuro-Linguistic Programming (NLP) teachers said to us during our training "If you don't know where you are going, it is very hard to get there." You might not know where you will end up, yet you need to have some kind of vision. What is yours? What are your dreams or aspirations? Many people seem to go through life without really finding out what they truly want from it, what makes them happy. Sometimes, they know but think that following their dreams is unfeasible or unattainable for many different reasons. We tend to think of dreams as unreal and elusive.

To achieve anything, you need to believe that it is possible and that you can pull it off. You are the one and only person here who can do it. Some dose of realism is necessary of course as some of our dreams are out of reach. I have found Neuro-Linguistic Programming to be a very helpful tool in mapping out and achieving goals and dreams in life. It offers many techniques that have proved effective in helping people set targets and reach them.

Once you have an aspiration, you can figure out the best way to achieve it according to your resources. With focus and trust that you will get there, your journey will be easier. A friend told me once that I was too focused on my destination to enjoy the journey. I now make a point of enjoying myself along the way.

Many of us don't know where to start when looking to make big changes in our lives. I have found it helpful to get a general idea first and then work on the specific details. There is an inspirational story called "Follow Your Dream" in "Chicken Soup for the Soul" which recounts how a young boy had a very specific and concrete dream he wrote about for a school assignment. Although the teacher threatened to fail him for his lack realism, he stood by his dream and later was successful in achieving it. The teacher actually admitted to him later on that she had stolen many dreams. Hold on to your dreams and all you need is for you to believe in it, no one else.

In the end, supporting yourself means giving yourself all the chances to be happy by following the path that inspires you and taking good care of yourself along the way. As we start to accept, appreciate and support ourselves, we are more able to do the same for others. Nelson Mandela used a quote from Marianne Williamson in his 1994 Inaugural Speech that is encouraging to me and I would like to share with you.

"Our deepest fear is not that we are inadequate. Our deepest fear is that we are powerful beyond measure. It is our light, not our darkness that most frightens us . . . And as we let our own light shine, we unconsciously give other people permission to do the same. As we are liberated from our fear, our presence automatically liberates others."

❀ PART II ❀

RELATING POSITIVELY TO OTHERS

CHAPTER 4

ACCEPTING OTHERS

IT'S EASIER ONCE YOU ACCEPT YOURSELF

My mother was an extremely critical person. She constantly judged people's looks, behaviors and beliefs. I had a great deal of trouble dealing with her incessant criticism of me while I was growing up. I never felt up to par around her. She had these expectations of perfection that were unachievable. What truly helped me deal with being judged all the time was the realization that she was her worst judge. She could never accept how she looked or who she was. She was constantly struggling because she could not come to terms with herself. It is hard to live in a skin you cannot bear. She applied the same harshness to everyone else and projected her own dissatisfaction on the world around her. As Don Miguel Ruiz recommended in his book the "Four Agreements", do not take anything personally. People have their own stories, which have nothing to do with you. I finally had to heed his advice and not take her judgments on board.

If people have become aware of their own limitations and imperfections and dealt with them with tolerance and understanding, they will be more accepting when they witness others grappling with theirs. Unfortunately, some of us are never able to drop the judge in our heads. As Ruiz also points out, "The Judge" can cause us much harm and truly hamper our quality of life. Being a judge sure made my mother miserable and damaged her relationships with her family. She hung on to "The Judge" until a few minutes before she passed away when she had a moment of clarity about her attitude. Her last words were: "I am sorry if I caused you (my brother and I) any harm; it did not mean to. All I knew was to obey laws and to judge". It is sad to think that it took a whole lifetime to come to such a realization. So much hurt could have been avoided if only she had dropped her critical and unsympathetic thinking.

When I trained to be a therapist, one of the main qualities we were required to communicate to our clients was that we were non-judgmental. We had to be accepting of all our clients no matter how we felt about them. Here was the other side of the coin. I had to treat everyone with tolerance. What a wonderful lesson for me to have to apply those premises. Because of my upbringing, I realized how tempted I was at times to be judgmental. It was a great exercise for me to break away from that destructive tendency. There were cases though where I was not able to take on a client because I could not deal with them as a person. I still had soft spots, which I needed to be aware of in order to make sure my clients were getting the best help possible. On certain occasions, I realized that I was not the most suited therapist for a client because of my own issues or my lack of expertise. I knew that in those cases it was better for my clients and for me to refer them out.

We all feel uncomfortable at times with other people's personalities and behaviors. Something about them seems to make you feel uneasy. You may not even be able to put your finger on what it is. If you need to be in close contact with that person, you may try to get them to change in order to feel better around them. However, I have learned over the years that people will not change their behavior just to please us. Even if we think that what we have in mind for them is so much better than the way they are, it is not up to us to make that call. In fact, if they actually try to change against their own will to accommodate us, it may not last or they may end up resenting us for forcing them to be someone they are not or acting in a way that is unnatural to them.

LET'S FACE IT, THEY WON'T CHANGE

How many times have I wished people in my life were different? I wished my mother were loving and warm. I wished my caregivers were kind and encouraging. I wished people in the world were more caring and tolerant of others. All of this was truly wishful thinking. I came to the sad conclusion after many attempts to make some of the people around me more caring, that I was fighting a losing battle. Unless they wanted to change, all my efforts were in vain. Some of them hung on to their ways even more as they felt threatened by this change I was trying to impose on them. I was infringing on their free will. I was attacking their freedom.

After a great deal of energy spent on these futile efforts, I realized that the people I was trying so hard to transform were not going to change for me. Accepting them the way they were was my only option. It did not mean that I had to be around them. It just meant that they were going to be who they were and the only choice I had a was whether I wanted to be in their company or not. There was a chance that they may eventually change but there was no guarantee that it would happen in the way I would like them to. I was basing my assumptions, as many people erroneously do, on the idea that because people love us they will be or act the way we wish them to.

I have found out the hard way that most people will actually resist pressures to change and that those attempts will create conflicts in relationships. The pressure of "if you love me, you would do this or be that . . ." does not work. You are no doubt infringing on someone's freedom to be who he or she is and do what he or she wants. They might try hard to please us at first but it probably will not last. There is also a high probability that they will come to resent having to be someone they are not or do something they do not want to do. Compromise is often necessary in our relationships with others whether it is when living together or working together. If people can find some middle ground that satisfies everyone, then a compromise is possible. However, expecting someone to change radically to suit our needs or desires is unlikely to be well received.

The French say "With "ifs", you could put Paris in a bottle". If only he/she was more/less this or did more of this or less of that. All those "ifs" can lead to a lot of frustrations. Again, looking for compromises may lead to extra effort on both sides to make things work. Compromising can prove very fruitful and constructive if it is done willingly and especially if it brings positive changes to all parties involved. However, if one person is pressuring another person through fear, guilt, withdrawal or angry outbursts, then the attempt to rally cooperation will most likely be, resisted or resented.

Once we have come to terms with the fact that others won't change for us, it is then up to us to decide if we are able to accept this person the way they are or not. If we don't, then we may choose not to associate with them. I realize that in certain situations, circumstances limit our choices. In families or in the workplace, we may have to have to be more accepting as we do not have the same leeway to avoid other people.

OPEN THE DOOR TO TOLERANCE

It truly saddens me to see how intolerant our world is today. Somehow, as our history shows, we have not been able to live peacefully together on this planet. We have had many opportunities to experience the horrendous consequences of intolerance through World Wars and numerous conflicts around the world throughout the ages. What are we missing? It would appear that we have not learned tolerance and cooperation. Is it not time for us on the brink of our own destruction to start thinking differently about how we approach each other and our environment? I sure hope so.

We need to become more accepting of others' differences and treat them with respect and caring. Shedding our many layers of prejudice will allow us to open ourselves to experiencing other perspectives and views. By choosing to be tolerant, we can open a whole new window on the world around us and have the opportunity to understand how and why others are actually different from us. Although we may not wish to adopt their perspectives, beliefs or approach to life, tolerance will facilitate peace and a better appreciation of our divergence.

How can we feel peaceful inside when we are full of anger and judgment for others? When we carry those emotions around, it becomes difficult to experience serenity and joy. Only by letting go of your fears and resentment will we achieve contentment. Now, how do we get there? It is a matter of changing the way we look at others. Let's say that right now, you are wearing red and black glasses (the most commonly used colors to describe anger). Now, if you switch them to pink glasses, you get a very different scene. Even though the scene has not changed, once you soften your outlook, it appears different. It seems softer because you have softened.

By adopting a gentle focus, you may begin to get a glimpse of the beauty of others. If nothing else, you will feel better about the whole scene, more at peace with it. As Mother Theresa said, "If you judge people, you have no time to love them." Indeed, if you have no inclination to love them, how can you discover who they truly are?

WALKING IN OTHER PEOPLES' SHOES

There is an old Sioux Indian Prayer, which encourages you to open yourself to other people's perspective before succumbing to the temptation of judging them without truly understanding their circumstances. It goes as follows:

> *Great Spirit, grant that I may not criticize my neighbor until I have walked a mile in their moccasins.*

We so often make assumptions or jump to conclusions about people without knowing much about them or their situation. My assumptions have been proven wrong many times. I am now a great deal more careful and I make a concerted effort to find out people's story before even trying to understand who they are and how they function. Once I have heard their story, then I try to imagine what it would be like to walk in their shoes. Have you ever tried to imagine what it would be like to be someone else, to be who they are and to live their lives? Getting into their shoes would shed a whole new light on what they are going through, how they feel and why they act the way they do. Having background information about them is not enough to fully grasp what their life is like. To imagine being them can be an enlightening process.

As a therapist, I have done my best to picture what it is like to walk in other people's shoes in order to relate to what my clients were experiencing. By entering into someone's world, I can get a better sense of where they are coming from. In this context, my world has no relevance to their situation; it only applies to mine. I have to remove my moccasins before I can slip into someone else's. Their world is a whole different universe of personality, circumstances, hopes and dreams, disillusions and traumas.

Ultimately, to truly accept another person, we need to accept first that they are walking in different moccasins.

One thing we all share is our emotions. We can relate to one another no matter what our respective stories are through our common experience of feeling joyful, hopeful, peaceful, discouraged, sad, angry, afraid or bereaved. Emotions are a common denominator between all human beings regardless of their personalities, background or circumstances. Studies among a variety of cultures have documented how we all display the same facial expressions when experiencing a specific emotion. We all share the same makeup when it comes to feeling. On that level, we can truly connect to one another and have compassion for each other.

LOOKING IN THE MIRROR

I have been asked on numerous occasions why I think relationships are so difficult. My response usually is that relationships are the main opportunities we have to learn about ourselves, and how we relate to others. This kind of learning truly stretches us by bringing to the surface all of our imperfections and issues and forcing us to become aware of them. Other people offer to us a reflection of ourselves. Through interacting with others, we learn about who we are, what we like and dislike about others and ourselves. Other people hold up a mirror for us so that we can identify who we are. We might not always like what we see. We may deny that this is our reflection or get upset with the person holding the mirror for tampering with the image we have of our self.

The people in our lives, depending on our relationship with them, hold up different mirrors for us. We can appear to be a different person depending on whom we are with. Most of us don't act the same way when we are with our parents or with our best friend or with our boss. The different roles we play, daughter/son, friend, mother/father, employee or teammate; all bring out distinct aspects of our personalities. As a result, we have a chance to see different facets of ourselves.

People we enjoy associating with usually possess similar qualities or attitudes to ours. As we share similar outlooks or values, we feel comfortable around them. Your friends therefore give you an opportunity to look at someone outside of you and recognize your own approach to life or people. By looking at who they are, we can get a glimpse of who we are and of why we choose to be with them. On the other hand, individuals we tend to dislike help us identify qualities or issues, which we find difficult to deal with or have an aversion to.

We have a great deal to learn from taking an honest look in all the mirrors that others hold up for us. It is a process of self-discovery. Some reflections may please us more than others, yet they all reveal a piece of who we are. When we hold a mirror up for others, if we do it with tolerance, they will tend to do the same for us. It can then become a positively reinforcing process that allows us to grow without being judged. This mutually positive feedback can help us improve ourselves in a safe environment and allow us to create bonds with others which are based on tolerance and understanding.

REACHING OUT

We are social animals by nature. It is in our makeup to connect with others and is healthy for us to do so. People who have good friends fare much better in life and feel better about themselves than the ones who don't. Relationships begin when we choose to reach out to one another. By making a conscious decision to be open and experience another person's reality, a whole other world reveals itself to us, a world of discovery and learning. To enjoy the experience fully, we need to be eager to learn about someone else. We need to be ready to listen with curiosity to the other person's story. This way, we may truly enter their world.

Actively listening to other people and trying to understand where they are coming from helps us become more receptive and tolerant of others. By giving them the opportunity to tell their story and by sharing yours, you will create trust and bonding. When you listen empathically and with a non-judgmental attitude, you reach out to the other person in a positive way. With some individuals, it may be harder than others. I had a strained relationship with my mother and communicating with her was, to say the least, challenging. The times when I felt the closest to her was when I listened to her story. She liked to go away with me when I was older as she loved to travel and was lonely. I had trouble finding something we could share during those times together as we had so little in common. The only thing I could think of was to ask her to share her story with me.

My mother was not a very communicative person. She was distant and cold most of the time. Yet, once I started truly listening to her with genuine interest and no judgment of any kind, she opened up. She revealed many details of her life. Some were very traumatic as she had been raised very strictly and had lived through the Second World War as a teenager residing alone in Paris. The city was occupied then and there was a curfew. She would hear gunshots in the night and lived in fear everyday. By hearing the accounts of her youth, I became more empathetic towards her and came to better understand the way she was. It allowed me to put our relationship in a different context. By reaching out to her in a positive way, I was able to get a glimpse of her world and transform my perception of her.

By truly listening, I was able to open the channels of communication. I made a real effort to hear her out, without judging her. I truly tried to see her life through her eyes. Although some of the choices she made, I still struggled with as they had caused me much harm, I saw her in a different light. Empathy begins by being sensitive to whatever the other person is experiencing. Unless you approach others with sensitivity and caring, you will not be able to really enter the other person's world deeply enough to understand their struggle or their joy. As Einstein said "Empathy is patiently and sincerely seeing the world through the other person's eyes. It is not learned in school; it is cultivated over a lifetime."

Reaching out to another human being is an opportunity to share of yourself with others and have them share themselves with you. In those moments, you realize that we can connect on a deep level with other people when we genuinely care to discover who they are and what their story is. We can recognize our universality and become closer to one another. As Carlos Ramirez wrote "What a world this would be if we just built bridges instead of walls".

HOLDING HANDS

When I was in primary school, we had to hold hands with another child and line up after recess to walk back into the school. I remember enjoying the closeness of holding a friend's hand. Touch was a sense I had not experienced very much as I grew up in an environment where holding a child was considered spoiling them. The world of tactile sensations was pretty foreign to me. It made the whole experience of holding my friend's hand while we waited in line so much more special. I knew then that connecting with others could be nurturing. To be held and to hold another took a great significance for me.

Many years later, I wrote a magazine article on the importance of touch for humans. Many studies have shown how babies who do not get sufficient touch have less of a chance to survive. We need to be nurtured and we need to nurture others. When I had my children, I made sure that they got a great deal of touch. We hugged, held hands and read stories in bed all bundled together. I learned baby massage and enjoyed connecting with my children through touch. It created such a feeling of closeness and bonding.

By touching someone else, we close the physical gap between us and we welcome intimacy. We let our bodies express what words often have difficulty expressing. Holding hands is a symbol of togetherness and peaceful union. It is a chance for us to recognize our similarities, our humanness, and our ultimate goal-to live together happily and peacefully on this earth. When you choose to reach out to another person, you embrace them as a person and reveal your willingness to accept them for who they are. As William Shakespeare wrote "Now join your hands and with your hands your hearts."

While holding hands, you can enjoy closeness and intimacy; you can give and receive warmth and caring; you can feel at peace with yourself and with others. You become connected. I like what Susan Jeffers wrote about embracing others: "Connection is made easier when we approach other people with the primary purpose of making them feel better about themselves." When we meet people with open hands and open hearts, we give them the opportunity to do the same. A mutually supportive connection can be made. As Steve Potter wrote "As a kid I learned that my brother and I could walk forever on a railroad track and never fall off-if we just reached across the track and held each other's hand".

CHAPTER 5

APPRECIATING OTHERS

OFFER PRAISE

I grew up in a culture that encourages critical thinking. To be able to think for yourself, you needed to be able to see all the flaws in an argument or a way of being. This intellectual approach offers a valuable method for developing discernment and one's own perspective. It can become destructive though when pushed too far as everything and everyone are constantly being scrutinized and assessed. When applied to individuals, excessive critical thinking can create deep insecurities. I asked my mother once why she always judged people so harshly. She responded that she did it for their own good. She believed that she was helping others improve by drawing attention to what they needed to work on.

Needless to say that when I was growing up, I was rarely praised. Yet, my faults were always pointed out to me. Again, this parenting approach was based on the premises that praising children would lead them to become spoiled and egotistic. Children do need however to be recognized for their value as unique and worthwhile human beings in order to develop a healthy self-esteem. Otherwise, they may spend a great deal of energy during their lifetime justifying their right to exist and proving their worth. On the other hand, if parents' compliments and encouragement are not genuine or overdone, they may lead to the development of feelings of insecurity in their children.

Children can sense when adults are not being authentic or have a hidden agenda for saying things. Nevertheless, when we honestly and caringly acknowledge another person's value, we communicate our true appreciation for them and lay the foundation for a positive and supportive relationship.

I feel that we always have a choice on how we approach people. Once we look for the good in them and focus on it, we feel much more positive overall. By showing our appreciation for others, we encourage open and constructive communication. Of course, there is no guarantee that our positive approach will be met favorably. However, I have noticed on many occasions that once you set a positive context for interaction, it makes people feel more comfortable and more willing to open up.

VALUING WHAT THEY DO

As I was sitting in a seminar yesterday, I noticed an interaction between two people, very similar to others I have witnessed many times before. Two participants sat down at the table in front of mine and introduced themselves. Then, the first question one of them asked the other was "what do you do?" It always amazes me how much individuals identify with what they do in our society. What you do defines you as an individual above all other things. Our occupations do take a great deal of our time. Many people's jobs though are far from being who they are. Yet, we tend to put a great emphasis on our professional activities and achievements as a way of identifying ourselves. What we do often appears more important than who we are as a person.

In our society, as different jobs have a different status, people tend to base their personal worth on the standing of their profession.

This hierarchy of roles tends to make us feel more or less valuable than the next person based strictly on what we do and how it is perceived by our society. I do not believe that the true value of an individual is determined by what they do but by who they are as a person. What they do is often an extension of who they are yet not always. I often wonder how many people have jobs that truly reflect their personality and their values. So many factors come into play in terms of what field we end up in, one of the most crucial especially right now being making a decent living.

Our activity, because it takes such a great amount of our time tends to have a huge impact on how we feel about ourselves. Many individuals take great pride in their achievements or status. They have put much effort in their work and it means a great deal to them. Recognizing and valuing what they have accomplished is important when expressing our appreciation for them. Showing genuine interest and giving positive feedback about their job is a constructive way to show our regard for them.

To truly appreciate others for who they are and what they do, we need to let go of our expectations and our opinion of what we think is best for them. It means respecting their choices and seeing the value in whatever they choose their path to be. It might mean letting others go down a path we believe will not be beneficial for them or more difficult than necessary. I know I have felt like screaming at times: "don't do it!", when I have had to stand by and watch friends, relatives or clients embark on journeys I felt were not going to work out or be more challenging than they needed to be. If appropriate, I would point out to them that they had other options. However, in the end, I had to let them pick their preferred choice and show consideration for their free will.

SEEING THE BEAUTY OF THEIR DREAMS

Eleanor Roosevelt wrote: "The future belongs to those who believe in the beauty of their dreams." To have a vision inspires us to reach for the stars, to become who we wish to be, to achieve the impossible. Dreams give us hope and motivate us to keep striving. For our dreams to come true, we need to believe in them. It does help if others support our aspirations as well. Dreams can be fragile and if others shoot them down, we may lose our motivation to pursue them. That is why it is so important to see the beauty in others' dreams as well as in our own.

Without dreamers, our world would lose some of its greatest visionaries and many of our amazing discoveries would have never occurred. When Don Quixote de la Mancha talks about his quest, he wants to "Reach the unreachable star and be better than he is, even if it brings him great pain and sorrow. Only if he attempts to fulfill his dream will he truly be able to feel peaceful and calm when he is laid to rest". I think that we all long to accomplish some dream, to follow our quest even if we know that it may be challenging. On our quest, we need others to cheer us on especially when it is treacherous.

Sometimes, when the journey seems long and tiresome and we lose hope, we need someone to have faith in us and remind us how important our dream is. Our friends and family cannot fulfill our dreams for us but they can be there all along, believing in them and encouraging us when we get discouraged. When I had doubts about writing this book, I would talk to my late friend Michelle. She believed in me so much and was so encouraging that I ended up following my dream. She could see the stars I was reaching for so clearly even when my vision got blurred. She was always able to perceive the beauty in my dreams and for that I am most grateful. It is a true gift to have people in your life that are always cheering you on from the sidelines.

SHARE YOUR HUMANITY

I have watched many of my relatives, friends, and clients go through difficult times in their lives. I used to think that if we became enlightened, we could escape suffering and grief. I have found that it is not the case. It seems that what we can do though is to become more accepting of the fact that they are a part of our lives. I remember talking to a colleague about it and he said that, as long as we are in a human body, we have lessons to learn and we will experience pain. I guess you could call those "growing pains". The human race still has so much to learn so we will keep feeling all the aches that go along being stretched and strengthened. As we all share this fate, we can relate to one another with understanding and empathy. We can share what it means to be human.

Appreciation has many definitions and one of them is "sensitive awareness". We can be aware and sensitive to the fact that people around us experience many challenges and suffering just like we do. Their circumstances may be drastically different from ours but the mental and emotional hardships they go through are similar. As I pointed out before, we all experience fear, anxiety, anger, grief, sadness, doubt and guilt. The fact that we all do is also an opportunity to realize how much we can be there for each other through it all.

People who have gone through challenging times together tend to build a strong bond as a result. It is often in those moments that our true humanity shines. When we face death or a traumatic event together, we get to a place where barriers between people come down. We are united by a common experience that is so powerful that it transcends all human separateness. We feel connected by our similitude. All walls come tumbling down and our true nature can be exposed and shared. Pain can take us into a depth of feeling that, as Omega Institute co-founder and writer, Elizabeth Lesser calls it, "breaks us open". It can bring us closer together and remind us how much we need each other through it all.

What often struck me during group therapy sessions was, how sharing their pain created a deep connection between people. I was impressed by how much caring and support was offered by the group members towards one another. On so many occasions I saw a true sharing of humanness. I was transformed by the experience and it gave me hope that we can develop or deepen our empathy for others once we let go of ours fears and our feelings of being different and separate. It gave me a glimpse of what our world could be like if we broke down the walls and shared our humanity.

RENEW YOUR TIES

I have lived in many places and met people from many different cultures over the years. Every time I moved, I had to leave behind dear friends with whom I had share meaningful moments, who had been witnesses and participants in important parts of my life. That was the hardest part about moving long distances-leaving people behind. It did not mean having to cut the ties between us; yet, it meant not being able to share as much of my journey with them. Relationships are what I value most in my life. I have realized over the years that the ties I have to the people I love cannot be broken by geography.

I am grateful for the wonderful friends I have made in my life. I have discovered that neither time nor distance has eroded my feelings for them. I am always touched by the appreciation we share for each other. It is the small gestures that often mean the most to me. A kind word, a comforting hug, a reassuring smile or a loving gesture lights up my world. As the English poet Samuel Taylor Coleridge wrote:

> *The happiness of life is made up of minute fractions. The little soon forgotten charities of a kiss or a smile, a kind look, a heartfelt compliment-countless infinitesimals of pleasurable and genial feelings.*

It does not take very much to build caring ties with others, only the intention to do so. There is always room to show how much we appreciate others. We can make a difference in people's lives by doing small acts of genuine appreciation such as words of kindness, smiles of recognition, embraces of joy or gratitude or being there to applaud or cheer. When we approach others with kindness and forgiveness, we consolidate our relationships and extend a renewed sense of appreciation towards others. Small touches can matter the most. We may never realize the difference we made in appreciating others but the important thing is that we do. As the Greek fables writer Aesop said twenty-five centuries ago, "No act of kindness, no matter how small, is ever wasted".

I value the opportunities to be of comfort to a friend in need. It is a chance to renew my genuine care for them and express through my words and my actions how much I care about them as a person. I received a message recently from a friend of mine thanking me for my help while her husband was fighting for his life. Although there was not much I could do for her, I expressed to her that I empathized with how difficult the experience must have been for her. Having lost people who meant the world to me, I could feel for her and wanted her to know that she was not alone in her pain. Sharing a common experience brought us closer together and I was able to recognize her need for comforting.

In some cases, the opportunity to renew ties comes at the end of people's lives when they sense that their time to go is near. In those moments, people often tend to look to make peace with their loved ones and their lives. It is unfortunate that it takes sometimes that long for people to realize the importance of appreciating others around them. One of my clients shared with me years ago that he had gone to see his father just before he passed away to finally tell him how much he cared about him. They had had a distant relationship and my client felt that he wanted to express his love for his father before it was too late. He told his dad how much he meant to him and for the first time, they had a heart-to-heart conversation, which left both of them feeling at peace and joyful. They had at last allowed themselves to reach out and communicate how much they loved one another. After that conversation, my client said how much easier it was for him to let his father go. Although in this particular case, they did not renew their ties until the very end, the earlier you can manage to do it, the more time you will have left to enjoy each other.

GRATITUDE FOR OUR TEACHERS

There is a saying that goes as follows: "There are no friends, no enemies, only teachers". I have tried to adopt this approach in my life although I have found it hard at times. When you feel hurt or angry as a result of what someone has said or has done, it can be difficult to remain calm and composed and remind yourself that there is something to be learned from the experience. When the lesson is hard, we tend to resent the teacher.

Some of my teachers were so easy to like and some so challenging. Today, I realize that I learned from all of them. The lessons, which taught me about negative emotions such as fear, anger, hurt, resentment and grief, were the hardest. I struggled through them, as we all do, and found it challenging not to perceive my teachers as the "enemies". I had to look very hard at times to see the learning in the situation. I would ask myself: why are they triggering these feelings in me? Why am I so upset? Which buttons are they pressing on here? What do I need to look at and work on? Once I got a better picture of what was going on with me, I could put the situation in perspective and diffuse it.

When you are faced with people or situations, which you find unsettling, upsetting or hurtful, do you ever wonder what issue they are bringing up for you? Are they some unresolved ones that you may find worth looking at and learning from? This is a chance to look at how you react and why and discover something about you. I have found that during those difficult lessons, adopting a grateful approach to your teachers, however difficult that may be, will make the experience easier to bear.

My teachers have all contributed to who I am as a person now. I am grateful to all of them although I still feel at times that my emotions want to get the best of me. When they do, I try to reframe the situation right away and look at why this is happening to me then. Our teachers enable us to look at the many aspects of ourselves and experience a gamut of emotions. Some, I honestly wish I had not had. Yet, they were all part of my growth and of my experience of what it means to be human. Even though I would have preferred to play only in romantic comedies on the stage of life, I learned so much more from the Greek tragedies. My instructors were much harder for the tragedies and they needed to be. I do appreciate all of them in the end for playing their part in helping me become who I am today: a stronger and wiser person.

OUR WONDROUS WORLD

When I watched Frank Capra's movie "It's a Wonderful Life", I marveled at how one man could have such a positive impact on others' lives. The main character, Gilbert, was a kind and generous man and had many friends because of his altruistic nature. He truly appreciated others and realized at the end of the movie how greatly appreciated he was in return. When he was in trouble, everyone he had been kind to, pulled together and helped him out. Once he rediscovered true appreciation in the midst of his troubles, he remembered how wondrous life could really be.

It is often during the hard times that we get a chance to realize how important it is to appreciate others for all their help and support and how much we can all do for each other. We are often so caught up in our own lives that we forget to be grateful for the people we meet and who make a difference in our existence. After I lost one of my closest friends early in life, I became painfully aware of how the ones I love could disappear tomorrow. I have learned from that experience never to take anyone for granted and to express my appreciation often. I value my friends so much more now.

I did not have a chance to say goodbye to my dear friend Raoul and if I could have had, I would have said so many "thank yous". I would have made sure I was grateful for every moment we shared. I would have thanked him for all the times he pulled me up when I was down and made me smile with his wonderful sense of humor. I would have made sure he knew that he was deeply valued. Maybe it would have helped him make peace with his life and realize how much he mattered to the ones who loved him. Maybe he would have then realized how wondrous life could be and would have stayed around a little longer.

Towards the end of "It's a Wonderful Life", Gilbert is given a chance to experience what the world would have been like if he had never existed. He discovered how much of a better place it was with him in it. People like Gilbert and the two best friends I lost truly make a positive impact on others' lives and deserve to be appreciated as real gifts.

CHAPTER 6

SUPPORTING OTHERS

BEING THERE

As a child when you stumble and fall, the first thing you do is look for your mom so she can make it all better. When my children were little and we lived in New Zealand, I loved hearing moms say: "come over here and I'll kiss it better" when their child fell off the swing or tripped on a branch. It was such a simple phrase yet it reflected so much caring and ever-present support. I still joke around with my children now and say it to them when they hurt themselves. Being the person who will always be there whenever they stumble through life is a privilege to me. To be someone else's rock is an amazing opportunity to show that you care.

During the tough times in my life, I have been fortunate to have a few people who supported me. They kept me going and believing that tomorrow could be better than today. It meant the world to me. Just knowing that they were there for me helped. Romantic poet, Samuel Taylor Coleridge said: "Friendship is a sheltering tree." There is no doubt that we all need shelter during our troubled moments. Knowing that there is a tree somewhere that will shelter us is deeply comforting.

What is the best way for us to offer support to others? Listening to others' stories and showing them that you care for them seems to be the most helpful. When we hurt, we need to be able to share our troubles and have someone let us express ourselves without interference or judgment. When we are listening to a friend's story, it can be awfully tempting to offer our own opinion on what we think is best for them. It has been my experience that most of the time, people want support not advice. They just want to be heard not told what to do. Ultimately, they need to figure it out on their own.

Funnily enough, I think that you can be overly supportive. I know that I have been too eager in the past carry others' burdens. I have now realized that as much as our relatives and friends need our support through the challenges they encounter, they also need to develop the skills to support themselves. In retrospect, I can see how I was not doing them any favor by allowing them to rely on me excessively. In the end, people need to develop a degree of self-sufficiency in order to find inner peace. Otherwise, they may become too dependent on external support and not build their inner strength.

EXERCISE KINDNESS

His Holiness the Dalai Lama said:

This is my simple religion. There is no need for
temples, no need for complicated philosophy.
Our own brain, our own heart is our temple; the
philosophy is kindness.

A few kind words can go a long way especially at times when life seems less than kind. If we all exercised more thoughtfulness and caring, we could transform the way we relate to one another at all levels. I have often been upset when I have realized the extent to which our world relies on competition. Winning habitually means beating one's opponent. During political campaigning, so many candidates use negative messages to make their opponent look bad instead of making themselves look good.

I have frequently wondered why human beings repeatedly hurt each other and keep on perpetuating a cycle of violence and resentment. Why haven't we learned to be kind? It sure seems like we have had many opportunities throughout history to learn that anger and oppression lead to pain and destruction. Is it the quest for power or survival that motivates us to crush our "perceived enemies" and hog the earth's resources? It has been shown that there is enough food for all yet so many go hungry. The desire to control and hold on to power actually comes from a deep fear for our survival. Our fears seem to lead to more fears and the cycle goes on.

It appears to me that only sharing and cooperation will alleviate our fears in the end, as we pull together towards a common cause. Giving and receiving need to become the core of our relationships for the welfare of all. Only by being caring and compassionate with one another, will we build better relationships. I have noticed how kindness is frequently mistaken for weakness. I have found the contrary actually. It does take great strength to remain gentle and humane when we are being mistreated. Turning the other cheek comes much harder that fighting back. We are programmed to fight or flee in the face of danger. Although in certain cases, we may need to fight for our lives, fleeing or diffusing the situation should be our first approach. When I trained in the martial arts, we were always told to walk away from a potential fight. Fighting was always meant to be a last resort.

Being caring and gentle can be particularly difficult when we are the target of an abusive individual. My mother was verbally abusive and I was on the receiving end of her putdowns for many years. I kept thinking that if I remained kind to her, she would eventually come around and soften up. As she got sicker and sicker at the end of her life, she became increasingly insulting and demanding. After turning the other cheek time and time again, I decided to walk away. I was not going to fight yet I was no longer going to put myself in a position where she could hurt me. Breaking away meant that she would no longer be able to take her anger out on me and I could be safe. Under certain circumstances I honestly think that it is the best thing to do. When I reached out to her again two years later just before she passed away, she was nicer to me. She had finally realized that she could no longer treat me harshly. I would no longer take it.

Throughout my life though, I have enjoyed wonderful friendships with people who were caring and giving. I have found that once you act kindly, it encourages people to respond with appreciation and benevolence. We have a choice to bring out the best or the worst in others. When we approach others with genuine and thoughtful attention, we create an opportunity to develop warm and positive relationships. Those make life so much more meaningful and enjoyable. Giving kindly to others benefit all. Twenty-five centuries ago, the revered Chinese philosopher Lao Tsu wrote about the virtue of giving:

The sage never tries to store things up. The more he does for others, the more he has. The more he gives to others, the greater his abundance.

A PROBLEM SHARED IS A PROBLEM HALVED

There is nothing worse than having to carry our burden alone. When we feel overwhelmed, scared or sad, sharing our troubles seems to lighten our load. In my practice, I have listened to many clients who needed someone to tell their story to. I was their witness and their support. I sat with them as they expressed their thoughts and their feelings. I validated their pain and offered empathy. I made sure that they knew that they were not alone in whatever trial they were going through. By telling their story, they were able to get some distance from it and often a different perspective. They were able to release some of the emotions that were bottled up inside of them. They often came to realize that others had gone through similar challenges before them and had come out stronger and wiser from them.

One response to suffering I have found frustrating over the years is when people told me when I was really hurting that it could be worse. Of course, things could have been worse. It did not take away the fact that what I was experiencing at the time was difficult to cope with. By minimizing my pain, I felt like people were taking away the validity of my feelings. It was almost a way of saying: "stop complaining, it's not that bad".

What truly mattered was how bad it felt to me then and how much I needed someone to say: "This is harsh, I feel for you".

Yes, suffering is relative and at times, widening our frame of reference can be helpful. There have been many occasions in my life where counting my blessings and putting things in perspective were helpful to me. Remembering what I had, helped me switch my outlook to a more positive one. Yet, we do not want to deny either the pain we are going through or pretend it away. It will only be repressed and will most likely resurface later. In the meantime, we will have to carry it around buried deep inside of us. Acknowledging it for what it is and expressing it will give it its true significance. It will also allow us to create some meaning out of the experience and learn from it.

I have found also that, events that can seem fairly benign trigger in us strong emotional responses. These are opportunities to revisit old traumas or sensitive issues and perhaps share some parts of our story that has been buried or too painful to talk about. After learning Time Line Therapy as part of my NLP training, I helped many of my clients go back into their past to identify specific events which were traumatic for them and caused them much difficulty through their lives. They went back in time and I was a witness to their story. They felt safe sharing those pieces of their lives and allowed themselves to observe the pain they went through and start their healing process. The fact that, they could safely share their suffering in a supportive environment, seemed to bring them great solace.

OPENING OURSELVES TO SUPPORT

Asking for help and accepting support from others puts us in a position of vulnerability, as we need something from someone else. Can we trust that they will be there for us and not hurt us in some way? Our ability to trust others comes from the very first years in our lives when we were completely dependent on our caregivers to take care of us. As babies, we need support for everything. We are in a position where our survival depends on others and we have to ask for food, warmth and love. We need to trust that those will be provided to us and that as a result we will survive. If we do not get our basic needs met a that stage in our lives, we will not develop trust and it will be difficult later on for us to trust that people will be there for us when we need them.

When I was taking a class on Human Growth and Development, I had a major breakthrough when I learned how important it was to have caregivers who we could trust to answer our cries as babies. I was finally able to understand why I was afraid to trust people. When I cried, no one would come. My mother told me many years later that my caregiver had advised her that, "it was good for babies to cry, it strengthened their lungs". It seemed absurd and very unnatural to me when I heard that statement. When I learned about the different stages of development in childhood, it validated my feeling about not tending to babies when they cry. Infants who are ignored when they cry out for their caregivers will have difficulty developing trust later on in life.

At a seminar I attended recently on "Attachment Issues", I was saddened to discover how many children in this country develop attachment issues as a result of non-responsive caregivers. According to current statistics, two-third of the North American population did not get the support they needed to strive as infants. This leaves us with a society that is full of people who learned that they could not trust others. I, like them, learned early on that there was no use in asking as nobody would care. When you ask over and over again and nothing happens, you internalize the fact that requesting won't help. So you stop asking and you learn to try to take care of yourself the best you can on your own.

Later on, when you need support in your life, you have trouble requesting it.

You feel reluctant to ask for support as you feel that you are burdening others with your personal problems or that nobody will really care to hear them out. And sometimes you will be right. Not everyone around you will be interested in being there for you when you need support. It has been my experience that people will surprise you both ways. Individuals you may have expected to be supportive will not be and others will be your rock when you never thought they would be. Most likely, your close friends who care about you will rally around you.

When we choose to offer support to others, we need to communicate to them that we will hear them out and not pass judgment regarding what they share with us. By setting a caring and trusting atmosphere, we can make the other person feel safe to share with us and lean on us. Also, by just letting them know that you are available if they need you, you allow them to feel free to come to you without feeling pressured about it. It may take time for some people to open up and they might even decide that they don't want to. Offering support is all we can do to help. Ultimately, it is up to them to take us up on our offer or not.

LEAN ON ME

As Bill Withers' lyrics go: "We all need somebody to lean on". His chorus sums up how much we need to support one another through the tough times: "Lean on me when you're not strong. And I'll be your friend. I'll help you carry on. For it won't be long until I'm gonna need somebody to lean on". I have learned about the value of support thanks to my two best friends and my brother. For when I needed them, they offered an empathetic ear and an open and caring heart. Without them, I would not have weathered some of the more difficult periods of my life. Thanks to them, I learned how important it is to have someone to lean on.

I have had many experiences in my life though where I needed support and I did not have any. What I found most challenging then was definitely not having someone to lean on. When I lost my closest friend in my early thirties. I had just fallen pregnant with my son and I lived far away from my family and childhood friends. I needed someone to help me through his tragic death. Ironically, I would have turned to him for support during times like these. He was gone and so was my main support. His loss was doubly difficult ad a result. I had to grieve him and I had to do it alone.

When I moved to England, I became very close friend with a wonderful woman who was a single mother like me. We leaned on one another and shared the most intimate details of our lives.

We were each other's rock through thick and thin for seven years. Shortly after I moved to the States, she passed away after months of illness. She was only 37. Again, I was living in a city where I knew nobody and had no support. And again, I had lost the one person who I could lean on.

Although we cannot carry others' burden for them, we can most definitely offer a shoulder to lean on. That shoulder can make a world of difference to someone who is struggling. By being comforting and empathetic in a non-intrusive and non-directing way, we can be the sheltering tree Coleridge described, to others, when the rain is pouring down on them. Over the years, I have supported many family members, friends and clients through their challenging times. What I found most important was to make sure that I had enough strength myself in order to be there for them. I needed to be aware of how much I was able to give to them before overextending. This is a common occurrence among therapists and leads to burnout.

When I started working as a therapist in New Zealand, I rented a room in a community center that offered health services and had my business line at home. At first, I was so excited about helping anyone who would call on me that I answered my business phone at all hours. I felt that I needed to launch my business and could not afford to miss a call. I soon realized that I was letting my work take over my life and that I needed to set clear boundaries between my home life and my work. I decided to set hours during which I would answer the phone and stick to them. Only in cases of emergency could people call my cell phone. I rarely gave it out. I learned to make sure I was supporting myself while supporting others.

Having others lean on you can take a great deal of your energy and you need to make sure that you are able to. When you are feeling tired physically or emotionally, it may be too taxing on you to help others. You may even become resentful of the other person for taking too much of your energy and attention. That becomes detrimental to both of you. Towards the end of her life, my mother used to call me up to four times per day for support. I was a working single mother and my time and energy were already tapped. Although I tried to explain to her that I could not be available whenever she needed me, she did not respect my time or space. Needless to say, that led me to feel imposed on and defensive. I think that it is important for us to be conscious of how much support we can offer before launching out to help everyone around us. Whenever I could, I have found supporting others in their time of need to be an enriching and gratifying experience. It also gave me the opportunity to develop strong bonds with other people.

Leaning on others can become counter-productive though if it goes on for too long. Being supported by someone else is like borrowing their strength when we don't have enough to stand on our own two feet. If we borrow it for a prolonged period of time, we risk not being able to carry ourselves anymore. We might become so dependent on the other person that we fail to rebuild our own strength. We need to remember that it is only helpful as a temporary measure until we regain our footing and our vigor.

FRIENDS UNTIL THE END

Friendships seem to transcend space and time. When I meet up with old friends I have not seen in years, it always strikes how we just pick up where we left off. The distance in years and geography has not changed anything. We are just as close and as happy to see each other as if we had been in contact everyday. Even if our existence are very different and we have not shared some of the important moments in one another's life for a long time, our relationship is intact and just as intimate as it used to be. Leaving good friends behind has been one of the most difficult things to do for me over the years. I often wish I could have all of my close friends living nearby instead of scattered all over the planet. The important thing is that they exist. Now, with the Internet, the world has shrunk and I can invite my friends and family into my living room over the airwaves. What a wonderful development.

The fact that feelings did not fade with time always puzzled me. One of my teachers twenty years ago told me "If you really love someone, you will always love them". Many years later, I can say that my feelings for the people I love have not changed. When I heard about the limbic system in our brain, which regulates emotions and cannot distinguish between today, yesterday or tomorrow, it all made sense. Our feelings truly have no sense of time. "I will always love you" did ring true. This realization was both comforting and disconcerting.

This meant then that the love I felt for others and they felt for me would live on. It also meant that monogamy was a difficult concept to apply. Can we love more than one person at a time has been a question I have been asked so many times. From my experience and all the stories I have heard, I would say yes. Our heart has many compartments and they house many different people and types of relationships. I could not say that I love my children any less because I love my brother or my friends. There is no quota in love. You have an infinite amount to give and share. Only fear can make us believe that there is a limited amount to go around.

The good news then is that our friendships can last a lifetime and we can keep making new ones. It has been particularly good for me considering how many times I have moved and had to start brand new friendships. Most of my old friendships have lasted over the years. Mutual support has been one of the most valuable aspects of these relationships. I have found that different friends have been there for many in different ways. People have distinctive means of offering support when you are going through difficulties. I have come to realize that not everyone has the strength or ability to be there for you in the way you may wish they did.

We may get disappointed that people we have supported in the past are unable to do the same for us. What we need to recognize is that not everyone is able to fill that role. It may be that they are going through a rough patch themselves or simply that they do not have the resources to do so. When rallying emotional support, I would pick very carefully. Your best supporter will be a person who is able to reach out to others and communicate empathy and caring and will have the time to be there for you.

SUPPORT COMES IN MANY WAYS

Some people are good at lifting your spirits by taking you out dancing or to a comedy show. Others will sit with you and listen as you pour out your sorrows. Others may give you flowers or chocolates. All of those are ways of communicating support. In general, it seems that people will offer the kind of support they are able to give or would like to receive if they were in a similar situation. I am always deeply touched when my friends reach out to me when I feel low. My friend Michelle had a knack for expressing empathy. She always knew what words to use to make you feel better and her voice communicated great warmth and caring. My friend Raoul used to make me laugh to cheer me up. He had such a funny take on situations that I would feel lighter simply from talking to him. My brother has a very rational and philosophical approach to human circumstances. He always helps me see the bigger and deeper picture in life. All three of them had distinctive styles in the way they offered support to me over the years and they were all extremely valuable to me.

Depending on what people are going through, they may need different types of support. How do we know what kind of help is best to offer others? How do we know how much to offer or when? I have found that most people welcome spontaneous giving when it is truly supportive and has no strings attached. Just expressing your desire to help and asking the other person what would be most beneficial to them seems to work best. It can be tough second-guessing what people truly need from us and

I have learned to inquire first in order to make sure that I was actually helping them.

I have come to realize that some people prefer to deal with things on their own and are not interested in unsolicited help or advice. I have learned to respect their ways of coping with situations and just made sure they knew I was there for them in case they felt they needed me. Before offering, I think it is wise to be clear about what we can give and how much. Imagining that we can rescue everybody is not feasible and not everyone seeks the support we can offer anyway. In the end, communicating our intention to be of help while being aware of our limitations and our boundaries will be the most effective and beneficial to all.

❧ PART III ❧

FEELING POSITIVE ABOUT LIFE

CHAPTER 7

FLOWING WITH LIFE

THE PATH OF LEAST RESISTANCE

If there is one thing I have learned, it is not to resist unnecessarily. How many times have I tried to resist situations to find out that it was a futile effort? It is amazing how much energy I spent in my youth fighting losing battles or the wrong battles altogether. Over the years, I have watched so many people exert themselves trying to influence others or have control over circumstances that were completely out of their control and end up feeling frustrated and defeated. I have definitely been one of them. After battling on for far too long, I would give up feeling exhausted and resentful. Fear motivates us to try to control everything and everyone. Trust, wisdom and strength will set us free from this absurd approach of swimming against the tide when we know that the tide is much stronger than us.

I remember getting caught in some strong breaking waves while visiting Hawaii many years ago and being tumbled forcefully. I could not get back to the surface to catch my breath. I was struggling to get out of the breakers and could not. I started to panic fearing that I was going to drown if I could not catch a breath soon. It was taking an incredible amount of energy to fight the waves that kept throwing me around. Finally, I relaxed and went with the rolling instead of against it and I was pushed towards the beach. I was safe yet very shaken by the experience. Going with the wave was the answer not against it. Yet, when we are scared, it is our first impulse to try to regain control even if it is counter-productive. Fear makes us hang on tighter; fight harder, when at times, letting go and releasing our grip will save us.

There is no doubt that relinquishing control can be scary. When we surrender, all kinds of anxiety-provoking questions arise: Where will I end up? What will happen to me? Will I be able to cope? Fear can be overwhelming and have a strong hold on us. We often set our minds on having situations turn out a certain way. When they don't, we feel let down and worried about the unexpected outcome. We might get a sense that we have failed or we may not have a back-up plan. We start to feel anxious at the uncertainty. The secret here seems to be: to have a clear intention of what we would like to happen and then let go of the outcome. This allows us to remain flexible and open to unexpected developments. It has been my experience that when I let go, situations work themselves out much better than I could have ever planned. It does not always appear that way at first. However, in retrospect, once I have assessed the situation within a larger context, it seems to have come together better in its own way.

When I arrived at eighteen in Los Angeles to start my undergraduate studies, I was all set to find a place to live and begin my college life. I did not realize that I had showed up very late to find a place to rent and could not get anything. I became discouraged and began panicking, as school was to start two weeks later. Walking around the campus, I became conscious of the fact that I did not like the place at all. I had never visited it because I lived so far away. Suddenly everything was falling apart and I had no clue what to do. I had no back-up plan and I was thousands of miles away from home. I met up with some friends of my family who suggested I go visit the college their daughter had attended and enjoyed thoroughly. When I set foot there, I knew it was perfect for me. By letting go of my original plan and being open to another option, I had found the best possible place for me. This seemingly disastrous situation proved to be a very positive learning experience for me.

On many occasions since then, I have attempted to remain flexible and mindful of the fact that there are so many other options we cannot perceive when making a decision. By releasing my need to control every outcome in my life, I have freed myself from my fears and been able to enjoy the journey a great deal more. British writer Stuart Wilde wrote:

> *Life was never meant to be a struggle just a gentle progression from one point to another, much like walking through a valley on a sunny day.*

I think that, we only know the point where we are now and we can make it easier on ourselves by letting go of the pressure of having to make it to our destination in a precise and controlled manner. This way we can actually take in the scenery instead of being obsessed with getting there.

TAKING IN ALL THE COLORS OF THE RAINBOW

The first time I remember seeing a rainbow was in California when I had just started college. I could not believe what I saw. There was a double rainbow outside of my dorm window. Having grown up in Paris, I could not recall seeing a great deal of sky out of my apartment window. I was in awe and felt like I was getting my own light show. I still have the pictures I took of that double rainbow. My friends, who had grown up in the area, were used to such a sight and did not pay much notice. For me, it was pure joy. Since then, I have lived in many places with beautiful skies and I have seen many rainbows. I still stop and soak them in and take photos. I am still captivated by their beauty and in awe at their vibrant colors.

Have you ever noticed how colors look different depending on the light? The same color can appear vibrant and alive on a sunny day and dull and lifeless on a grey one. All those shades make up the incredible range of our palette of experiences. Every single one offers a distinctive and unique experience in itself. They all contribute to create the richness of our lives.

Even when the sky does not light up to give me sparkles of colors, I look around for all the beauty that surrounds me. I make a point of taking in all of what life has to offer me on this planet in this lifetime.

Learning meditation in my early thirties was particularly helpful to me in becoming more aware of each instant and slowing down my mind. It was hard at first to keep my thoughts from rushing around and the whole experience seemed somewhat frustrating.

After twenty years of meditating, I find it less challenging and I truly appreciate it as a wonderful way of stopping everything and appreciating just being. Practicing mindfulness has taught me to value the here and now and to be present in every moment. As a result, I can truly enjoy every single instant in my life. I can let go of the past and not worry about the future. I just take the time to be.

Now, what about you, how do you take in the colors of the rainbow? How do you make sure that life does not pass you by without ever appreciating the world around you? When you look at all the facets of your life, which ones bring you the most joy and satisfaction? By observing each one carefully and letting yourself enjoy them to the fullest, you will have the opportunity to live a deeper and more satisfying life.

FAVOR LIFE

There were plenty of times in my life when I felt less than positive. Even after I discovered my three golden keys: acceptance, appreciation and support; my life did not fall into place perfectly. I have done my best to hang on to those keys and open as many doors in my heads with them as possible. They have overall made my circumstances more manageable and indeed more positive. Even at my lowest points, I always favored life. The other alternative was pretty dire. Favoring life though meant more than simply being alive. It meant embracing life the best I could by searching for the good and the beautiful wherever I could find it.

I have always loved nature and animals and whenever I observe them closely, I always notice that no matter what, they strive to live life to its fullest and give it all the energy they possess. By observing plants and animals, I have learned how the true nature of any living creature is to make the most of their environment and circumstances. We are all programmed to fight for our survival and to tap into our inner resources to keep us going. As challenges present themselves to us, we learn about ourselves, about others and about how to live the best way we can. The many bumps and bruises we carry around prove that although we may have been toppled over many times, we still got up and continued to learn and experience all that our existence had to offer.

I was told once the journey was not meant to be easy. Only by experiencing all of the facets of life, could we truly appreciate it in its wholeness. When I look back, I can say that the hard times have made me appreciate the good ones and the hard teachers I had taught me valuable lessons. I have grown stronger and wiser in the process and I have more compassion for the struggles others go through. I now approach life as an adventure with my three golden keys as my guides. I have become increasingly able to remain positive in whatever comes my way. My life has truly become positively different as a result.

ACKNOWLEDGEMENTS

Revising this book has been a wonderful experience for me. It has been an opportunity to realize how much I have learned and grown over the last ten years. When I think of the people who inspired me and encouraged me, the list is long. My family, my friends, my teachers and my clients have all contributed to the many insights I shared in this book.

My two best friends, Raoul Modecke and Michelle Taylor will always be my greatest inspiration even though both of them have passed away. Their influence in my life was immense. They showed me what love, compassion and kindness looked like and felt like. It was a real honor to have them in my life even if it was for too brief a time.

My brother Gilles has always kept me mentally stimulated and has been a wonderful emotional support. I am so grateful to have him on my side. My father Michel Colin has also been extremely encouraging and supportive and it has meant a great deal to me.

My children, Tasha and Sean, have been an amazing source of enthusiasm, curiosity and encouragement for me. I am delighted and thankful to my daughter for designing the cover of this book and grateful to my son for cheering me on throughout the many hours spent on this project. They both personify my golden keys.